B-52 stratofortress in action

by LOU DRENDEL

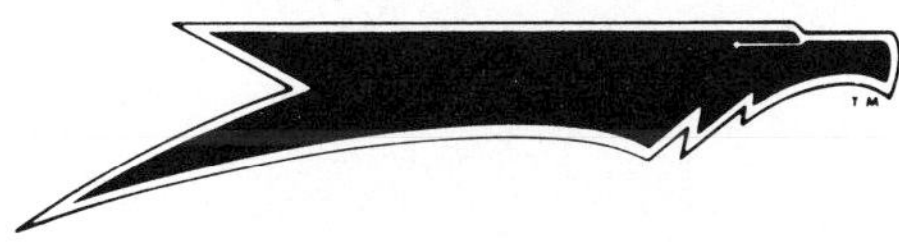

squadron/signal publications

Acknowledgements: A lot of people put a lot of time and effort into seeing to it that I got maximum support in putting this book together, and I feel obligated to thank them in print for their unflagging support. As always, Lt. Col. Shirley Bach, Chief of the Magazine and Book Branch, SAFOI, got me pointed in the right direction. At SAC Headquarters I was warmly received by their chief IO, Colonel John Walton, who put me in the able hands of my long-suffering escort, Capt. Art Forster, who shepherded me through the extensive briefings provided by SAC and saw to it that I got on and off the B-52 at Blytheville AFB. Ken Buchanan surrendered up his entire collection of slides for me to pick and choose from, and Chuck Mayer allowed me to do likewise with his photos and personal memorabilia collected while serving in a B-52 wing. And, of course, a lot of other private collectors did the same. Their names appear under many of the photos herein. My profound thanks to one and all.

LD

Other "in Action" Titles

by Lou Drendel

Gunslingers in Action
A-7 Corsair II in Action
B-52 Stratofortress in Action
F-15 Eagle in Action
F-104 Starfighter in Action
F-14 Tomcat in Action
F-111 in Action
F-5 in Action
C-130 Hercules in Action
A-10 Warthog in Action
F-16 Fighting Falcon in Action
SR-71 Blackbird in Action

by Lou Drendel and Capt. Don Carson

F-106 Delta Dart in Action

[Cover] B-52D of the 43rd Strategic Bomb Wing, flown by Major Bill Stocker leads mission of 26 December, 1972. Airborne mission commander Colonel James R. McCarthy rides in IP seat.

COPYRIGHT © 1975 SQUADRON/SIGNAL PUBLICATIONS, INC.

1115 CROWLEY DRIVE, CARROLLTON, TEXAS 75011-5010

All rights reserved. No part of this publication may be reproduced, stored in a retrival system or transmitted in any form by any means electrical, mechanical or otherwise, without written permission of the publisher.

ISBN 0-89747-022-2

If you have any photographs of the aircraft, armor, soldiers or ships of any nation, particularly wartime snapshots, why not share them with us and help make Squadron/Signal's books all the more interesting and complete in the future. Any photograph sent to us will be copied and the original returned. The donor will be fully credited for any photos used. Please send them to: Squadron/Signal Publications, Inc., 1115 Crowley Dr., Carrollton, TX 75011-5010.

Photo Credits

USAF
NASA
Norman E. Taylor
Paul Stevens
Kenneth Buchanan
Charles B. Mayer
Lou Drendel
Boeing

Introduction

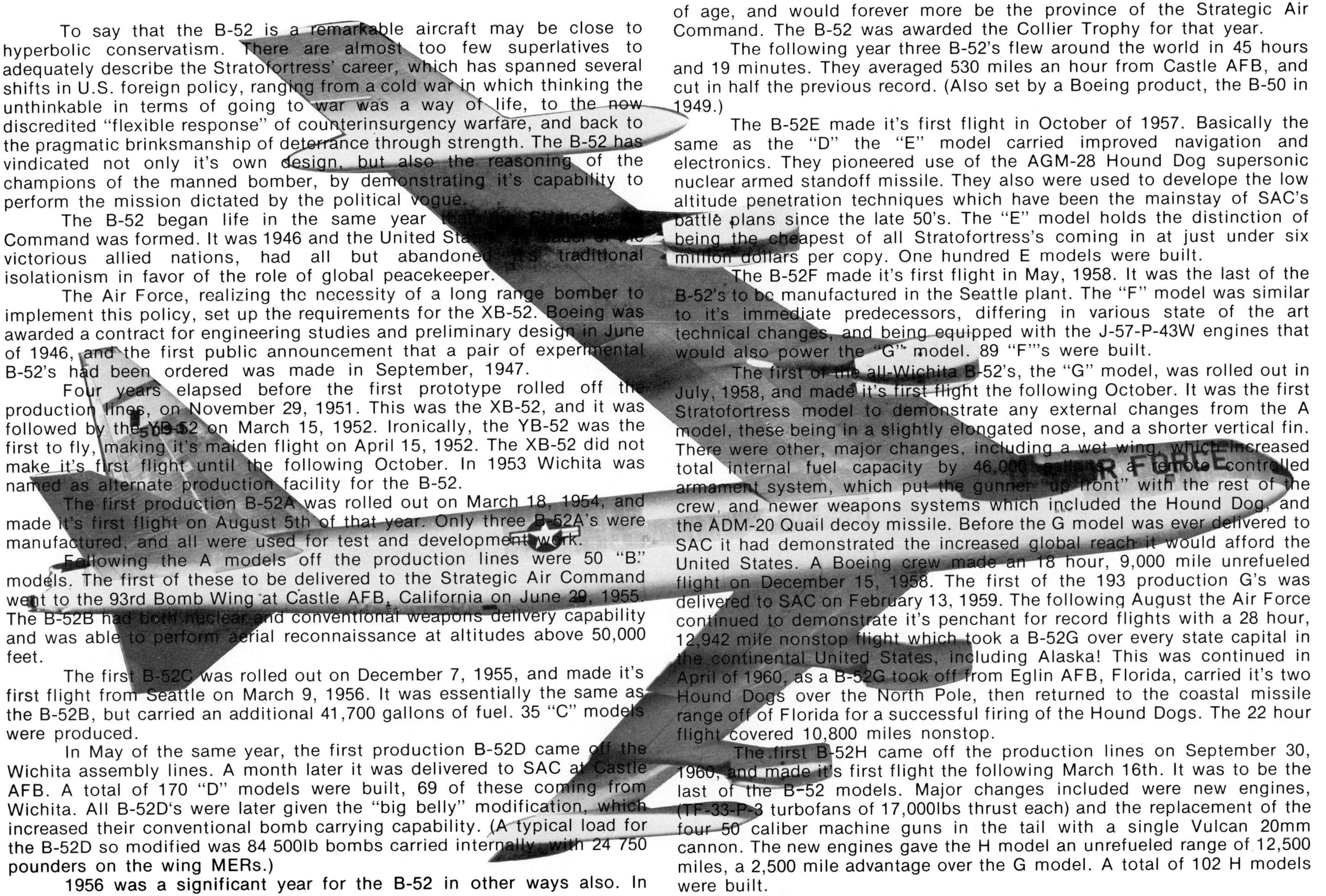

To say that the B-52 is a remarkable aircraft may be close to hyperbolic conservatism. There are almost too few superlatives to adequately describe the Stratofortress' career, which has spanned several shifts in U.S. foreign policy, ranging from a cold war in which thinking the unthinkable in terms of going to war was a way of life, to the now discredited "flexible response" of counterinsurgency warfare, and back to the pragmatic brinksmanship of deterrance through strength. The B-52 has vindicated not only it's own design, but also the reasoning of the champions of the manned bomber, by demonstrating it's capability to perform the mission dictated by the political vogue.

The B-52 began life in the same year that the Strategic Air Command was formed. It was 1946 and the United States, leader of the victorious allied nations, had all but abandoned it's traditional isolationism in favor of the role of global peacekeeper.

The Air Force, realizing the necessity of a long range bomber to implement this policy, set up the requirements for the XB-52. Boeing was awarded a contract for engineering studies and preliminary design in June of 1946, and the first public announcement that a pair of experimental B-52's had been ordered was made in September, 1947.

Four years elapsed before the first prototype rolled off the production lines, on November 29, 1951. This was the XB-52, and it was followed by the YB-52 on March 15, 1952. Ironically, the YB-52 was the first to fly, making it's maiden flight on April 15, 1952. The XB-52 did not make it's first flight until the following October. In 1953 Wichita was named as alternate production facility for the B-52.

The first production B-52A was rolled out on March 18, 1954, and made it's first flight on August 5th of that year. Only three B-52A's were manufactured, and all were used for test and development work.

Following the A models off the production lines were 50 "B" models. The first of these to be delivered to the Strategic Air Command went to the 93rd Bomb Wing at Castle AFB, California on June 29, 1955. The B-52B had both nuclear and conventional weapons delivery capability and was able to perform aerial reconnaissance at altitudes above 50,000 feet.

The first B-52C was rolled out on December 7, 1955, and made it's first flight from Seattle on March 9, 1956. It was essentially the same as the B-52B, but carried an additional 41,700 gallons of fuel. 35 "C" models were produced.

In May of the same year, the first production B-52D came off the Wichita assembly lines. A month later it was delivered to SAC at Castle AFB. A total of 170 "D" models were built, 69 of these coming from Wichita. All B-52D's were later given the "big belly" modification, which increased their conventional bomb carrying capability. (A typical load for the B-52D so modified was 84 500lb bombs carried internally, with 24 750 pounders on the wing MERs.)

1956 was a significant year for the B-52 in other ways also. In August preliminary authorization for the "G" model was given, and in November eight Stratoforts completed record nonstop flights of up to 17,000 miles, on routes which carried them over the North Pole. One of these aircraft was in the air for 31½ hours! Aerial refueling had truly come of age, and would forever more be the province of the Strategic Air Command. The B-52 was awarded the Collier Trophy for that year.

The following year three B-52's flew around the world in 45 hours and 19 minutes. They averaged 530 miles an hour from Castle AFB, and cut in half the previous record. (Also set by a Boeing product, the B-50 in 1949.)

The B-52E made it's first flight in October of 1957. Basically the same as the "D" the "E" model carried improved navigation and electronics. They pioneered use of the AGM-28 Hound Dog supersonic nuclear armed standoff missile. They also were used to develope the low altitude penetration techniques which have been the mainstay of SAC's battle plans since the late 50's. The "E" model holds the distinction of being the cheapest of all Stratofortress's coming in at just under six million dollars per copy. One hundred E models were built.

The B-52F made it's first flight in May, 1958. It was the last of the B-52's to be manufactured in the Seattle plant. The "F" model was similar to it's immediate predecessors, differing in various state of the art technical changes, and being equipped with the J-57-P-43W engines that would also power the "G" model. 89 "F"'s were built.

The first of the all-Wichita B-52's, the "G" model, was rolled out in July, 1958, and made it's first flight the following October. It was the first Stratofortress model to demonstrate any external changes from the A model, these being in a slightly elongated nose, and a shorter vertical fin. There were other, major changes, including a wet wing, which increased total internal fuel capacity by 46,000 gallons, a remote controlled armament system, which put the gunner "up front" with the rest of the crew, and newer weapons systems which included the Hound Dog, and the ADM-20 Quail decoy missile. Before the G model was ever delivered to SAC it had demonstrated the increased global reach it would afford the United States. A Boeing crew made an 18 hour, 9,000 mile unrefueled flight on December 15, 1958. The first of the 193 production G's was delivered to SAC on February 13, 1959. The following August the Air Force continued to demonstrate it's penchant for record flights with a 28 hour, 12,942 mile nonstop flight which took a B-52G over every state capital in the continental United States, including Alaska! This was continued in April of 1960, as a B-52G took off from Eglin AFB, Florida, carried it's two Hound Dogs over the North Pole, then returned to the coastal missile range off of Florida for a successful firing of the Hound Dogs. The 22 hour flight covered 10,800 miles nonstop.

The first B-52H came off the production lines on September 30, 1960, and made it's first flight the following March 16th. It was to be the last of the B-52 models. Major changes included were new engines, (TF-33-P-3 turbofans of 17,000lbs thrust each) and the replacement of the four 50 caliber machine guns in the tail with a single Vulcan 20mm cannon. The new engines gave the H model an unrefueled range of 12,500 miles, a 2,500 mile advantage over the G model. A total of 102 H models were built.

Preparing the XB-52 for it's first flight. Tandem seating arrangement is most evident in this photo. Pilot for this flight was the famous Tex Johnston, who is in front of cockpit. [Boeing]

Cockpit Detail

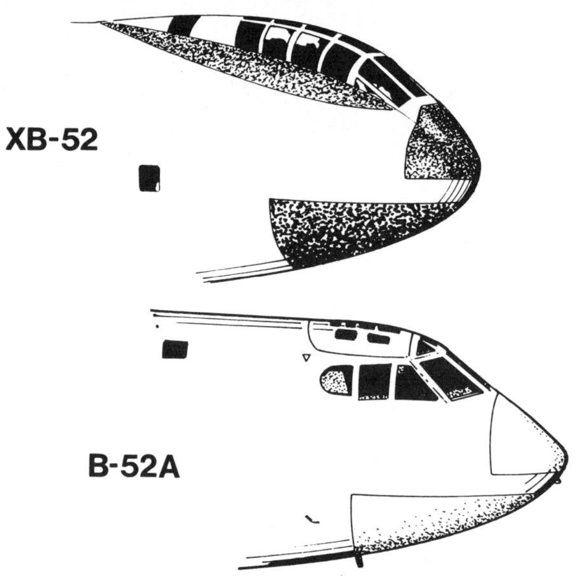

YB-52 takes off on it's first flight. YB-52, though completed 3½ months after the XB-52, flew 5 months before the XB-52. YB was the first Stratofortress to fly. [USAF]

YB-52 with it's SAC predecessor, the B-47. YB-52, though much larger than the B-47, was a much less critical aircraft to fly. Photo taken at Seattle in May, 1954. [USAF]

Secrecy [and a big blanket] shrouded the rollout of the XB-52 in the middle of the night of November 29, 1951. [Boeing]

First operational B-52 leaving Moses Lake, Washington enroute to Castle AFB, California. [top] Delivery ceremony [below] has BG Wm. Eubank, Jr. accepting first B-52 from Boeing officials on June 29, 1955. [Boeing]

First operational B-52 now resides peacefully in Strategic Air Command Museum at Offutt AFB, Nebraska. [Author]

Early B-52D cockpit layout. [Boeing]

Instrument panel and right side console of a currently operational B-52D. Changes from early models are confined to state-of-the-art refinements in radar and instruments. [left and below. Photos by the author]

XB-52 demonstrates one of the radical design features of the Stratofortress . . . it's crosswind landing gear. Yes, it is coming straight at you! [Boeing]

XB-52 [top] and RB-52B [below]

Lots of midnight oil was burned at Boeing in the initial phases of B-52 production. 88 B-52A, B & C models were produced at Boeing's Seattle facility. [Boeing]

No, it's not a fugitive from Railroader Magazine. This is the traveling B-52 simulator, photographed here at Blytheville AFB, Arkansas. Center section contains the cockpit, while cars at either end hold power units and briefing room. [Author]

B-52F-BW of the 736th BS, 454th BW, taking off from Columbus AFB, Miss. 6 Sept. 1967. It carries a pair of Hound Dog AGMs. [Charles B. Mayer]

B-52E pioneered the low-level delivery techniques that are SAC standard for going-to-war-under-the-radar today. It is shown here along the Washington coast. [Boeing]

Hound Dog Missile under the wing of a B-52D. AGM-28 was 42 feet long, carried a 4 megaton nuclear warhead, and could cruise for 600 miles at mach 2. It entered SAC service in December, 1959. [Boeing]

B-52D-80-BO at Edwards AFB in May, 1962. It is christened "First Lady of Glasgow" [Arnold Swanberg via Norman E. Taylor]

Kelly AFB, Texas was the specialized maintenance depot for the B-52. Here a B-52D undergoes refurbishment. Note the fold-down vertical tail. [USAF via Norman E. Taylor]

Evolvement of B-52 defensive armament; All models through the "D" positioned gunner in the tail. A through G models used a battery of four radar directed fifty caliber machine guns. H model introduced the 20mm Vulcan cannon, capable of 4,000 rpm rate of fire. In G and H models, the gunner sits in front of aircraft, next to Electronics Warfare Officer. Defensive design philosophy was vindicated [to a certain extent] in combat, as B-52 gunners claimed two confirmed Mig Kills. No B-52's were lost to enemy fighters. [Author and Boeing]

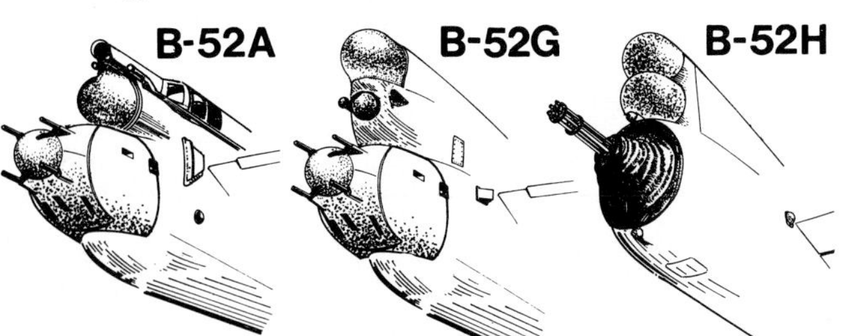

Armament Detail

RB-52B-10-BO Serial number 52-8714 ["O" prefix on tail number designates the aircraft as being obsolete, a practice the Air Force instituted to identify aircraft that had ten years of service. With many active duty aircraft approaching their twentieth birthdays, it is no wonder that the practice has been discontinued.] Photographed at Chanute AFB, Ill. in May of 1965 by Roger Besecker. [via Norman E. Taylor]

B-52D-35-BW, serial number 56-0675, of the 92nd Strategic Aerospace Wing. Fairchild AFB, Washington, May, 1970. [Norman E. Taylor]

B-52H 60-0028 of the 716th BS, 449th BW, based at Kincheloe AFB, Mich. was photographed at Kelly AFB in March, 1973 by Norman E. Taylor. Note open drag chute door behind tail.

Crew of B-52G answers scramble call during alert exercise. Hound Dog Missiles are camouflaged to match bombers that carry them. [USAF]

B-52H moves into precontact position behind KC-135 tanker in pre-camouflage cold war days. [USAF]

B-52G during landing approach. White paint used on undersides of Stratofortress is heat reflective and is designed to shield the bomber from effects of nuclear flash. [Boeing]

B-52H going through IRAN at Kelly AFB. Crane has just removed ejection seat. Open nose affords excellent view of radar. [Norman E. Taylor]

B-52D launching ADM-20C Quail decoy missile. Quail was designed to imitate the B-52 on enemy radar screens. Electronics ensure a radar return equal to that of the B-52, and it can be programmed to simulate B-52 attack profiles. Up to four Quails could be carried, and they had a range of 250 miles. [Boeing]

Brand new [at the time] B-52G refueling from a venerable [even at the time!] KC-97. [Boeing]

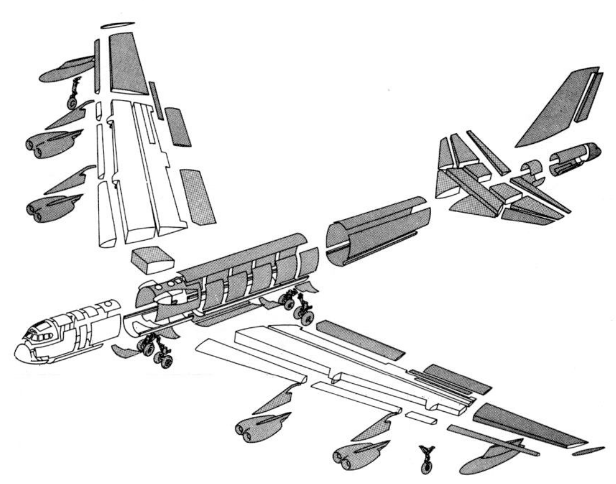

Exploded view of B-52 indicates components built by Boeing, [white] and those subcontracted to others. [shaded] [Boeing]

It takes a whole lot of nylon to slow a B-52 down! [Boeing]

One-of-a-kind overall gloss white paint scheme was applied to this B-52G before it's assignment of USAF Flight Test Center at Edwards AFB. The white paint is highly visible over the desert, and helps to deflect some of that desert sun, keeping electronics and crew cool. [Boeing]

Tail Detail

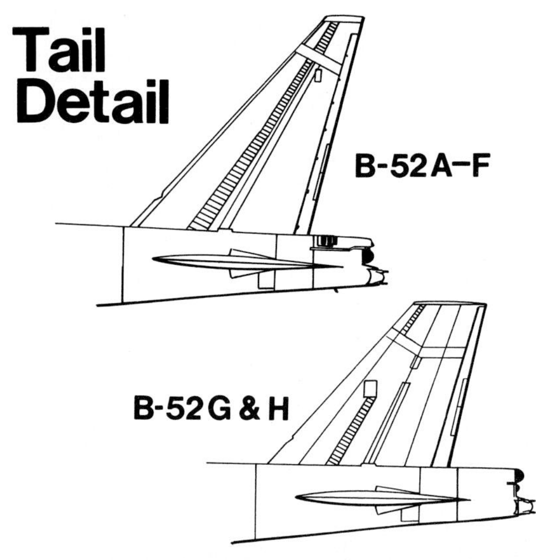

Rollout of last B-52 produced ocoured in 1962. [Boeing]

B-52H of the 34th BS, 17th BW, "City of Fairborn" [Ohio] took part in McCoy AFB Bomb Competition. [Ken Buchanan]

B-52D-35-BW Serial No. 56-680 of the 367th BS, 306th BW was the hometown entry in McCoy Bomb Comp. Ironically, it is also the B-52 flown by Bill Stocker on the 26 December, 1972 Hanoi raid. [See story "Linebacker II"] [Ken Buchanan]

SAC's bombing competitions bring together the best aircraft and crews of each unit. The aircraft used are individualized by the unit artist, who is obviously not allowed to use WWII heavy bomber artwork for reference. [All photos by Ken Buchanan]

SAC bomb competitions have been held since 1948. They were instituted in response to a general decline in post WWII bombing proficiency. Begun as an annual event, the "World Series of Bombing" is now held as budgetary and operational committments allow. They are hosted by operational SAC bases. B-52's have participated since 1956. [All photos on this page taken by Ken Buchanan at 1970 & 1971 McCoy AFB competition.]

All phases of B-52 operations are scored in competitions, including weapons handling and loading. Note special smart uniforms worn by members of this 68th BW crew. [USAF]

Blytheville AFB competition entry was named for famous B-17. [above] [USAF] "Wilbur" was entry from Wright Patterson in McCoy competition. [below] [Ken Buchanan]

Testing... **Testing...**

Testing...

NB-52A Serial number 52-0003 with the X-15. All three B-52A's were eventually assigned to test duties within the Air Force. [USAF via Norman E. Taylor]

X-15 under the wing of "The High and Mighty One". In latter stages of X-15 program, the rocket ship was equipped with additional fuel tanks. [Boeing]

NB-52B carries the badge of Air Force Systems Command on it's nose. At Edwards AFB, May, 1972. [Duane Kasulka via Norman E. Taylor]

[Below] Two views of NB-52A X-15 carrier. Photo at top taken in 1965, shows large accumulation of missions on scoreboard. [side of fuselage] Also, note name below eagle; "The High and Mighty One" [Duane Kasulka via Norman E. Taylor] Bottom photo taken very early in X-15 program. [Note X-15 nose gear extended] [Boeing]

Two views [top and bottom] of the X-15 drop at 42,000 feet. B-52 was ideally suited to mission of carrying X-15's and Lifting Bodies to high altitudes for launch. [Boeing]

Termination of X-15 testing did not spell the end of operational test use of NB-52's. Here they are seen carrying the X-24B [top], and the M2-F2 [bottom] lifting bodies to altitude. Lifting body research is aimed at finding best aerodynamic approach to the Space Shuttle. [Boeing]

B-52D, Ser. No. 56-0636 was used as test bed for the Pratt & Whitney JT-9D Fanjet engine developed for use on the Boeing 747. It provides remarkable visual evidence of powerplant advancement. [Pratt & Whitney via Norman E. Taylor]

B-52H refueling from KC-135 during testing of Skybolt Missile System. Stratofortress carries four dummy Skybolts under wings. Skybolt was the forerunner of the SRAM. It did not achieve operational status. [Boeing]

B-52H with Skybolts during testing. With the cancellation of the Skybolt, the H model began carrying the Hound Dog Missile. B-52 was able to carry full complement of internal weapons in addition to four Skybolts. [Boeing]

Control Configured Vehicle NB-52E sported the most colorful paint job of all B-52's, with bright red forward fuselage, vertical fin, engine nacelle trim, wing tanks, and fuselage stripe. CCV embodied Ride Control System which reduced accelerations caused by gust turbulence by up to 30 %. Features of the system visible in these photos are the horizontal and vertical canards on the nose. Testing of the system began in 1973, under the direction of the Air Force Flight Dynamics Laboratory. Funding of 4.6 million dollars will allow extensive R & D of the RCS. B-52 was chosen as ideal large aircraft for study, while F-4 Phantom was chosen as smaller aircraft test bed. [Boeing]

Rotary Launcher for SRAM

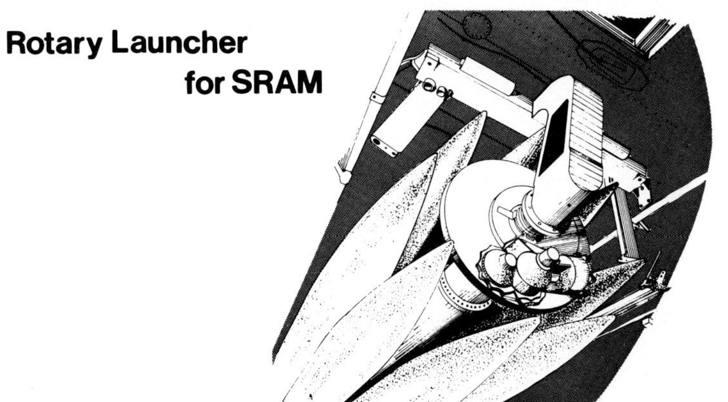

Test B-52G being escorted by F-86 chase plane. [Boeing]

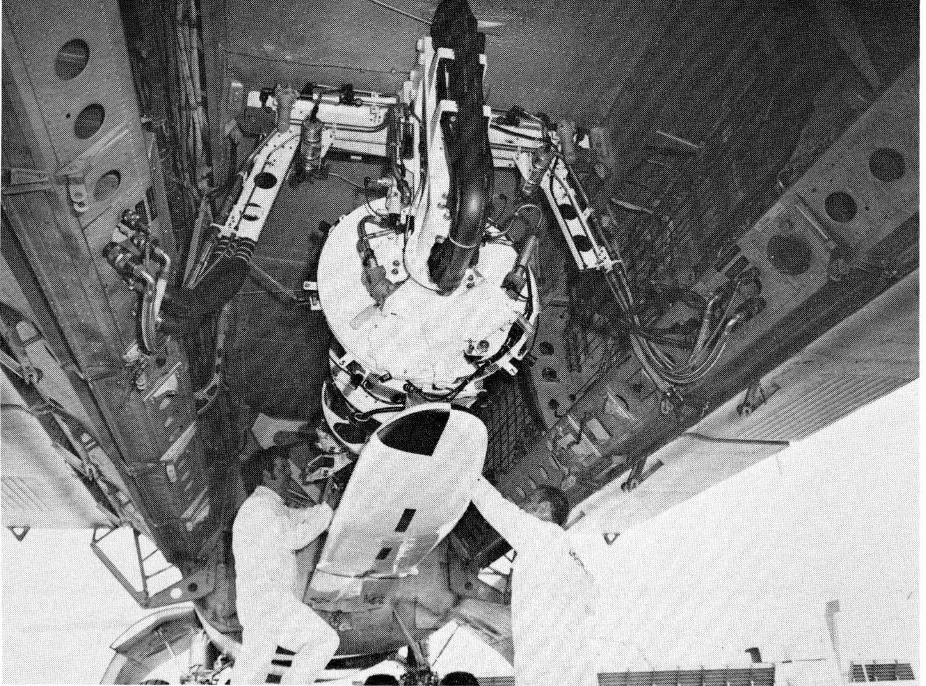

Air Launched Cruise Missile being loaded in bomb bay of B-52H at Boeing's Wichita plant. Missile was later successfully launched from B-52 flying over White Sands, N.M. Missile Range. [Boeing]

NB-52A Ser. No. 52-0003 lifts off from Edwards AFB, California with the X-15 underwing.

B-52D shows off SEA combat camouflage pattern as ground crew loads it for a mission. [USAF]

B-52D cockpit [Author]

B-52H 60-0008 of the 19th Bomb Wing, 8th AF as it appeared during bomb competition at RAF Markham, England, 1967. Inscription on fuselage reads; "Dear Rocky, not to win is a very bad thing." Despite this admonition, none of the three SAC representative crews managed to bring home a trophy.

Hound Dog equipped B-52H shows off pre-camouflage era paint scheme of aluminum and gloss white. [USAF]

Over-the-shoulder look at the left seat of a B-52G. [Author]

Combat

As a result of the success of conventional bomb operations in 1965, all B-52D's were "big belly" modified to increase their conventional bomb capability up to 57 %. The modifications were done at Boeing-Wichita in 1966 after a one month test period in which two 52's made 31 flights and dropped 1,497 bombs on ranges in Kansas and Florida. [Boeing]

B-52F's on Guam await loading of 750 lb. bombs.

B-52F of the 454th BW approaches a KC-135 tanker for pre-strike AR. Guam based B-52's required several refuelings to cover the 5,000 mile-plus round trip from Guam to Vietnam. First B-52 raid was flown in June 18, 1965, with 27 B-52's hitting a suspected Vietcong concentration in War Zone D. Two 52's were lost in a mid-air collision north of the island of Luzon. [USAF]

Two of 28 B-52's releasing their bomb loads on VC staging area 30 miles from Saigon, during July 7, 1965 missions. [USAF]

B-52F Ser. No. 57-034 named "Parker's Pride" [after Wing CO Parker] On ramp 8, Andersen AFB, Guam, 31 March, 1966. Only major modification to B-52's which took part in 1965 and early 66 bombing campaign was the conversion of Hound Dog pylons to conventional bomb carrying capability. [Charles B. Mayer]

B-52F SN 57-164 454th/320th BW, Andersen AFB, 5 March, 1966. Named "Connie's Competition". Though tradition of naming aircraft was continued from previous conflicts, it was ground crews who named aircraft on Guam, since flight crews seldom flew the same aircraft often enough to feel a particular kinship with it. External ordnance loads added considerable weight to wings and made job of handling 52's in flight that much more difficult. Normal gross takeoff weight was about 450,000 lbs. [Charles B. Mayer]

"Chain of Thunder", a B-52F-BW SN 57-142. 454th/320th BW, Andersen AFB, March 1966. [Charles B. Mayer]

External bomb loading on "Chain of Thunder". Note weathering of black paint on undersurfaces, and short pylon, which can be compared to normal long pylon [below] used on B-52F. [Charles B. Mayer]

Brigadier General Jimmy Stewart [the same!] walks away from B-52F SN 57-149 after participating in a mission against the VC in 1966. [left] [Charles B. Mayer]

"Lady Luck" was first B-52 to rack up 100 missions. She was a B-52F-BW-65 SN 57-139. [Charles B. Mayer]

Team which loaded 50,000th bomb in B-52 campaign poses with aircraft which carried it. [B-52F-BW-65 SN 57-152 "Casper the Ghost"] They are congratulated by Wing CO Col. Van R. Parker. [USAF via Charles B. Mayer]

View from the front office of a B-52D entroute to the target. Normal mission time from Guam to Vietnam and return was 12 hours plus, and often covered more than the straight-line distance of 5,000 miles, due to diversionary feints. Early 52 missions were navigated without the aid of Loran or TACAN, relying on celestial navigation to find their way to Vietnam and return. [USAF]

B-52D in Southeast Asia combat livery. Two-tone green and tan upper surfaces, with full size "USAF" and national marking. Gloss black undersurfaces and vertical fin. Serial number on fin is red, while stripe and number on wingtank is in white. [USAF]

B-52D loosing a load of 500 lb. bombs. Big Belly modified "D" is capable of carrying up to 108 iron bombs. [USAF]

Loading 500 pounders on the short pylon under a B-52D wing. Principle modification was the addition of an "I" beam to the pylon. A pair of standard MER's is then attached to the I beam, with a capacity of 12 500 or 750 pound bombs. [USAF]

Preloaded 500 pound bomb "clips" allow fast loading of the Big Belly "D" bomb bay. [External bombs must be loaded individually.] [USAF]

A pair of B-52D's returning to Andersen AFB after a 1967 mission. [USAF via Norman E. Taylor]

B-52D rolls out, post mission. Size of huge flaps and position of wing-top lift spoilers is most evident. [USAF]

Maintenance logistics on the B-52 are complicated by it's behemoth size. [USAF]

Bomb damage assesment photos [below] show the devastation caused by B-52's. Concentration of bombs, coupled with lack of forewarning, made the B-52 one of the most feared weapons employed in Vietnam War. [USAF]

Anderson AFB, Guam became a literal sea of B-52's during the Linebacker campaign, reminiscent of the great B-29 armadas assembled during WWII in the Pacific. Both "D" and "G" models were employed. [USAF]

Linebacker II

After 17 years of SAC service, the B-52 finally laid to rest any doubts which might have lingered about it's ability to perform the strategic bombardment mission. During 11 days in December of 1972 the B-52's penetrated the strongest air defense network ever encountered in the history of aerial warfare to put their loads precisely on target.

The targets were military and industrial complexes in the Hanoi/Haiphong area of North Vietnam. They were struck as a result of a continuing intransigence and faithless bargaining position of the enemy, and to demonstrate to the enemy that the United States had the means and the will to do whatever had to be done to negotiate the return of POW's, and an end to hostilities in Southeast Asia. That the enemy was in the end dishonest in his signing of a so-called "peace agreement" demonstrates beyond any doubt that if he had had the means to effectively resist the aerial onslaught of Linebacker II, he would have done so. For 11 days out of 11 years, the United States was anything but a paper tiger, as bombs rained virtually around the clock on the enemy homeland.

While at Blytheville AFB, Arkansas, I interviewed Brigadier General James R. McCarthy, who is now commander of the 42nd Air Division. During the Linebacker II campaign he was Wing Commander of the 43rd Strategic Wing, based at Andersen AFB, Guam. He was one of the planners of many of the B-52 raids during that campaign and won the Air Force Cross as Airborne Mission Commander, flying in the lead bomber, on the spectacular mission of 26 December, 1972. These are his recollections of the Linebacker II campaign:

"I think if you really want to see the significance of these raids, from an airmanship standpoint, you have to go back in history and compare them to some of the big raids of World War II. For the Ploesti raid, as an example, a complete mockup of the target was built in the Lybian desert, and the bomber crews practiced and practiced, and practiced. Our raid of December 26, 1972 employed improved tactics. We had never practiced them at all. (Author's note: In many of the big raids of World War II, such as Ploesti, Regensburg, and Schweinfurt, losses of 20 to 30% were experienced. The overall Linebacker II losses were about 2%.) The tactics were very complex, and the timing was plus or minus zero. Normal SAC crew training is plus or minus three minutes. This had to be zero. From that standpoint alone . . . to go up and do it the first time around, without ever having had the benefit of practice, and to do it with some pretty junior, inexperienced guys flying, was pretty fantastic. As an example, I had one pilot who, on his fourth mission as an aircraft commander, flew

this mission . . . at night, over North Vietnam. That's calling for a hell of a lot out of a guy, and he did it, and did a fine job!

There was a lot of controversy about whether you should be allowed to maneuver or not. A B-52 is not like an F-4, for example. With an F-4 you could tuck it in close and fly a pretty good formation while maneuvering. A B-52, on the other hand, is very hard on the controls, so it takes a lot of physical power and coordination to wrassle it around the sky . . . . . sort of like driving a Mack Truck. On the third night, we really got zapped bad, so as a concerted effort the command developed new tactics. We had been attacking from the northwest, down Thud Ridge. After hitting the target, we would make a hellacious turn to get out of the area. That gave us the minimum time in the lethal SAM zone. When an area is as heavily defended as Hanoi/Haiphong was, the lethal zone was pretty large. Naturally, you don't want to spend any more time in that environment than is absolutely necessary. Well, all of our losses seemed to stem from that big turn, so tactics which eliminated the big turn wherever possible were developed. (Authors note; Another bone of contention was the fact that these "new" tactics were not introduced until the sixth night of the 11 day campaign. This was not due to any lack of insight on the part of the commanders. It was more a result of the length of the missions. For example: The mission of the 19th would only be returning when the mission of the 20th was taking off. The distance from Guam to Vietnam made these some of the longest, if not **the** longest in the history of aerial warfare, sometimes lasting up to 18 hours. The 20th mission would be well on their way to the target before the previous day's mission had debriefed. This, in effect, doubled the lead times needed to change tactics.) Well, we knew we had to do something about that big turn, and we knew we had to stop driving in the same way every night. After all, those radar operators could just about draw a grease pencil line on their scopes, they knew our routes so well! The 36 hour stand-down for Christmas gave us the breather we needed to come up with new tactics.

The tactic SAC came up with was for four waves of B-52's to hit four targets, which were relatively close to each other, in the Hanoi area, while other B-52's attacked targets in the Haiphong area. All of these attacks were to be carried out simultaneously. Many of the older B-52D models struck the heavily defended areas around Hanoi. This was ironic, and I can recall thinking as we flew up that night how thankful I had been, back in 1960, when I transitioned to the B-52, that I was flying the B-52E instead of those tired old D models. And here I was, taking four waves of those old D's, twelve years later, to the toughest targets we had ever attacked! Another change we made that night was to vary the altitudes we flew at. We were attacking the Hanoi railyards, while the wave which came in from the northwest was attacking a target just three miles away! True, they were at a different altitude than we were, but we were attacking simultaneously. The targets being struck by the two southern waves, one from the southeast and one from the southwest, were only seven miles away, and they too were being struck simultaneously. The biggest fear we had was one of the bombers in the high waves being hit and falling through our wave.

At this point I'd like to go back to the beginning of the Linebacker II campaign. It was eight days before Christmas, and a lot of the crews were scheduled, through normal rotation, to go back and spend Christmas with their families. In addition, we had worked out a plan whereby we could send extra crews home by doubling up on some of the flying. Well, when the word on Linebacker II came down, I had to call a meeting of all of the aircraft commanders. I told them that everyone was restricted to the base, that they were not going home, that they were not allowed to make any telephone calls, and that we were going to fly some extremely important missions.

Well, I had seventy-some crews, and as is normally the case, four of five were DNF (Do Not Fly) because of colds or sinuses, or other minor ailments. The first question I got after breaking the news was; "Sir, those of us that are grounded...do we have your permission to try to talk the flight surgeon into letting us fly?" Well, that showed me a lot, and before the campaign was over, they gave me many more reasons to be proud of them. There were three B-52 wings participating in Linebacker II. The 43rd, which I commanded, the 307th, which was based at Utapao RTAB, and the 72nd, also based at Andersen. The 43rd and the 307th were the "D" wings, while the 72nd flew the "G" models. During the entire operation, I did not have one guy who refused to fly, and when it was all over, we had the lowest loss rate of any of the B-52 wings. Naturally, we wanted to know why, and conducted a "monday morning quarterback" session after the campaign was over.

We had stressed mutual protection, distaining the hellacious types of manuevers some guys were making in an attempt to dodge the SAMs. You can't dodge a SAM. At least, not in a B-52. A lot of guys thought they could, and a lot of them tried. But we stressed basic air discipline, keeping the formation together. This takes a lot of guts, because the miss distance the system is designed to give you makes it virtually impossible to tell if the SAM is going to fly right up your nose, or miss you. So for a bomber pilot to keep boring in, straight and level when the SAMs are all around, takes a lot of intestinal fortitude. That's not the same as a fighter. In a fighter, you could wait until the missile was within about a click of you, then break down into it. In a fifty two you couldn't do that...the airplane couldn't take much of that kind of G force. So I told my troops: "If you break formation to dodge a SAM, I'll court-martial you!" Now, that didn't go down too well at first, but after about four days they were coming to me and admitting that it was the best way . . . . . we were losing less airplanes, and getting our bombs on the targets better. Now, if a guy starts dodging SAMs, he not only highlights himself, he degrades the ECM effectiveness of the formation. We recovered one crew that was shot down, and the pilot admitted that he had been breaking left every time a SAM was fired at him. The first night he got away with it, and thought he had the answer. Well, on the third night the SAMs were heavier, and he kept breaking left until he was about five miles out of the formation. He got zapped.

Now, we did maneuver some, but it was a very gentle maneuver, and it kept the formation together. One of the advantages of the D model manifested itself here. We gave the tail gunners Aldis Lamps, and with their radar they could pretty well tell where the trailing bomber was. When we maneuvered, the gunner would flash his lamp to let the following B-52 know which way to turn. And, if we kept the formation together, the burner cans of the eight engines were visible to the trailing B-52. This made a great attitude indicator, and we got so that we could make these

Refueling Receptacle

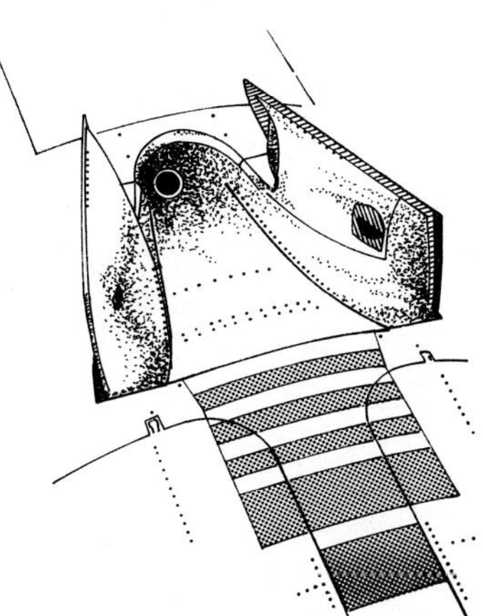

Tension personified...faces of B-52 crewmen mirror their feelings as Hanoi is announced as the target for the first time. 18 December, 1972. [USAF via Major Bill Stocker]

B-52D ready for a mission. Weathering of camouflage is an indication of the maintenance difficulties caused by the tropic air. [USAF]

maneuvers and still keep the formation intact. This was no mean feat, since many of those nights were moonless, and a lot of the guys were relatively low-time pilots. (1200 hours total time, with maybe 300 in the B-52) Now, you expect that kind of flying from a guy with four or five thousand hours, but to get it from inexperienced pilots is really fantastic! I attribute our success to their training, their native intelligence, and to their attitude.

As for that training; at Andersen we had a requirement for two "over the shoulder" missions, one in the day and one at night, with an experienced aircraft commander and radar navigator, to make sure that he had the procedures down, before we let them go as aircraft commanders on their own. That was if he was doing good refueling. A lot of the G and H model pilots had trouble transitioning to the D. It was a much harder airplane to fly, particularly with bombs hanging on the external racks. And it had less power than the G and H models, so the average guy might take three or four missions to get qualified in the D.

There was a significant change in attitude as the campaign progressed. Initially, I had a lot of guys come up to me and say; "Colonel, I don't mind telling you . . . I'm really scared!" I'd have to tell them; "Don't feel like the Lone Ranger, friend!" And here is where the value of having the wing commanders fly the missions really paid off. I'm from the old school. I believe a commander should be in the thick of it, leading his troops.

We, as high ranking officers, had a lot of information that the enemy would dearly have loved to get and, normally speaking, we should never have been allowed to fly. But we discussed it, and decided that the value of the information was not as important as the morale factor which our flying would have. On every mission that we launched, we had an airborne mission commander, who had to be a full colonel, and a deputy airborne mission commander. We took our turns on these missions, the duties being split between the Wing Commanders, their Vice Commanders and the DCO's.

The low point, attitude wise, was just before the Christmas stand-down. We had lost a lot of airplanes, and then giving the enemy a chance to get set for us on the 26th really had the guys worried. But our tactics were more effective than we could have hoped they would be. By the night of the 28th we noticed that the SAMs were far less accurate. They would launch them in salvoes, and they appeared to be unguided, coming up and going every which way. By the 29th the crews were saying; "Don't stop now! We've got this thing won. Another week of this, and we can go up and do it in the daylight!"

The pilot of one of the crews who was shot down, and later recovered, told me how he was shot down. They were within seconds of bombs away when they picked up the SAM launch. This was the most critical part of the bomb run and they knew if they wavered, their bombs would be off target. They had all of the electronic indications that the SAM was indeed aimed at them, and in fact, they picked it up visually. It never wavered for a second . . .it's relative position in the windscreen was constant as the rocket motor exhaust grew larger and larger. They knew it was going to hit them . . . in fact, one of the calls on the intercom just before it hit was; "This one's gonna get us!" It did. Just after bombs away. But they put their bombs on the target, and that's what I call "guts football". Fortunately, they were able to bail out, and were recovered later.

The tremendous attitude of the crews was matched by the support people. Many times I saw bomb loaders or maintenance men work their own shifts, then stay on to help their buddies on the next shift. And when we took off on those missions we often had 15,000 airmen out there on the line, cheering us on. It was a tremendous team effort, and I can't tell you how impressed I was by those young kids who, sensing the importance of these missions, and knowing how many lives were on line, really worked their hearts out for us. It was a historic chapter in aerial warfare, and I'm glad to have had the chance to participate.

The mission of 26 December, 1972 was a turning point in the Linebacker II campaign. It was a turning point for the B-52 crews because the tactics greatly enhanced their effectiveness, allowing them to penetrate the enemy defenses with less chance of getting hit. It was a turning point for the North Vietnamese because it delivered a psychological blow that they were not equipped to handle.

The B-52 had long been one of the most feared weapons by the North Vietnamese. Colonel Robinson Risner, a POW of the North Vietnamese for seven years, stated that the enemy was not afraid to fight the fighter-bombers. The fighters came in low. They could be seen, and the enemy could fire at them with small arms. Even if they didn't hit the fighters, they could see them and they felt they were able to resist. The B-52's came over at night, and at high altitude. Often the enemy never knew he was under attack until the bombs started falling. And the bomb load of a B-52 is awesome. (Up to 60,000 lbs in the D model.)

On the night of 26 December, 117 B-52's hit their targets within 13 minutes. It was a cataclysmic experience for the North Vietnamese. One of the POW's later told General McCarthy that he had observed an enemy guard during the raid. The guard was standing in the compound staring at the sky. He had dropped his rifle and was shaking like a leaf, and he had wet his pants.

Major William F. Stocker flew the lead B-52 on this raid, and he was awarded the Silver Star for leading the mission. I interviewed him at Offut AFB, and these are his recollections of the mission; "During the Christmas stand-down we didn't really know if we would have to go back to war or not. We were all hoping that they would get together at Paris, and come up with some sort of an agreement. On Christmas night General (Colonel at the time) McCarthy invited several of us to his home for dinner. We all enjoyed a real nice dinner, and we were relaxing over a drink afterwards, when the guests began to thin out. General Anderson was the first to go. He was the Division Commander, and we were still pretty busy recycling aircraft and crews, so we didn't think much of it. Then Colonel McCarthy got up and announced that he was going to have to leave also. He urged us to stay as long as we liked, and to help ourselves to his bar . . . "All except you, Stocker. You're coming with me."

When we got outside he broke the news to me that we would be going back to Hanoi the next day, and that I would be leading the mission and he would fly with me. He asked me to go down to the D.O.X. (the planning area), and to look over the mission profile. If I saw anything that should be changed, I should get back to him and iron it out.

I'll never forget the feeling of incongruity as I worked with the planners that night. I had dressed for the social occasion, and was wearing white slacks and shoes and a brightly colored shirt I had had made in Thailand. I was a sharp contrast to the uniforms around me, and the contrast highlighted the urgency of this mission.

The complexity of the actual attack created heretofore unheard of logistics problems. The number of airplanes going required a massive logistics effort. We had never sent a raid that large at one time, and we didn't have a briefing room large enough to hold all of the crews. As a result, we had to use several facilities, and the briefers had to go from one to the other, giving their portion of the briefings. Food service had never had to prepare that many flight lunches at one time, and they really had to work long and hard to accommodate all of us. Just to taxi that many airplanes at one time...to keep them all in the proper sequence, and to make sure that spares were in position to go if an airplane aborted, was a major feat of planning.

Normally, we made a rolling takeoff, turning the corner from the taxiway and starting right into our takeoff run. But since I was leading, and they had sterilized the runway, allowing absolutely no traffic, I requested permission to taxi into position and hold, awaiting my time out. They granted it, and in the minute or so before we took off, I was treated to the sight of one of the most awesome armadas ever assembled. As far as we could see there were B-52's lined up nose-to-tail. It's difficult to describe the feeling of leading such an array of power.

Shortly after takeoff, I heard a good friend of mine, who was trailing me on the launch, call an emergency. Captain Jerry Goodman called in with two engines on fire. Naturally, he had to abort, but the ordeal of the next few hours matched anything he would have gone through in the target area. He was diverted out over the ocean to burn off fuel and get down to minimum landing weight. (We had no provision for

Concertina wire protects the flight line a Utapao RTAB from would-be sabotuers. Arc Light missions against enemy troop concentrations were supplemented in 1972 by Bullet Shot, which introduced the first real strategic bombing effort to the Vietnam War. [USAF]

Crew Chief directs a loaded D from it's parking space at the beginning of a mission. Ground crews regularly worked 12 and 14 hour days to keep the BUFs flying, yet morale was at an all-time high, as 8th AF posted the highest career re-enlistment rate for SAC during the 1972 bombing campaigns. [USAF]

Liftoff for a 16 hour mission against communist targets in North Vietnam. [USAF]

dumping fuel.) During his orbit the other two engines on the same side caught on fire, and he had to shut them down. He got permission to jettison his bombs into the ocean, and did so. As is so often the case, one problem was compounded by another shortly thereafter. As he was cranking in the rudder trim to hold against the four dead engines, it broke! This is very rare...I had never heard of it's happening, but our airplanes were old, and the corrosive atmosphere of Guam didn't help in trying to maintain them in top condition. He and his Co-pilot adjusted their seats for maximum leverage, and between them managed to stand on the rudder pedal hard enough to keep the airplane flying straight. (Not an easy job...there is at least 80 to 90 pounds of pressure.)

The people at Andersen talked it over and, considering the possibility of his dinging it on the runway, and concerned about all the returning airplanes they would have to recover, decided it would be best if he bailed out and let the airplane go. Jerry argued against this and convinced them that he could land it safely. When he was down to minimum landing weight, he began his approach. (Minimum landing weight in the B-52D is 280,000 pounds.)

At one time it had been considered a real bad idea to try to land the B-52 without flaps...there just didn't seem to be enough runway available to get one stopped without them. But eventually someone had to try it, having had an engine blow up, which damaged the flaps and made them inoperable. After he got down, he reported that it was not nearly as bad as it was made out to seem, and that if he had to land with three or four engines out on one side, he would prefer to do it flaps up, since he would have less drag and more power to work with. Well, they did some studies on that, and decided that he was right. The technique was installed as an optional procedure.

Jerry was flying a D model, which has less available power than any of the B-52's. The book says it doesn't have enough power with four engines out to make a go-around, if you get below 2,000 feet AGL. On his first approach, Jerry was too high and too hot, but rather than force the landing, he coolly made the decision to go-around before he descended below 2,000 feet. On his second try he got it down and stopped safely. He was awarded the Distinguished Flying Cross for a superior piece of airmanship.

We had a set air refueling area which, due to political considerations and civil air routes, could not be changed. In all of our previous missions the position of the sun had not been a problem or, if it was, the area was large enough to allow slight alterations of the tracks. But with a strike this large, there was no room for maneuver, and we were forced to refuel into the sun. I had anticipated the problem and had made myself a cardboard shade, with a window cut in it, to block out the sun. By leaning a bit to one side I was able to get my gas without too much trouble, but we were very concerned about how the young crews would handle this situation.
Well, they handled it tremendously well, and I didn't have a single plane that didn't get his gas.

A little by-play that occurred during the launch illustrated the size of the force, and the time required to get it airborne. As I was in departure, a commercial airliner called Agana Approach Control. (Agana is the commercial airfield on Guam, and was the only other concrete available, so they were holding it open in case of emergencies.) His conversation went something like this; "Agana approach, this is Pan Am flight so and so. Request landing instructions, over." "Pan Am, this is Agana. Descend to one zero thousand, proceed south and orbit at 70 miles, 180 degree radial, Agana, and say your endurance fuel." "Agana, this is Pan Am. We have...ah...3½ hours fuel...Do you have an emergency?...How long a delay can we expect?" "Pan Am, this is Agana. You can expect up to a 3 hour delay. No emergency. Tactical considerations!" His reaction was spontaneous, and unprintable.

Our first big decision on whether to abort the mission was caused by tanker problems. A tanker cell which was supporting the

Local visibility was sharply reduced as the B-52's filled the skies over Andersen with black exhaust with their one minute interval takeoffs on Linebacker II missions. [USAF]

B-52G returns from strike as a B-52D taxies out for beginning of a mission. Graphic evidence of the constant activity required for support of Linebacker II missions! [USAF]

bombers was delayed twenty minutes because on an emergency situation at Kadena. By all rights, this should have caused a mission scrub for one or two of the bomber cells. We felt that, going up against the targets we were attacking, it was of the utmost importance to have all of our briefed bomb tonnage. We had taken off one minute apart, five minutes between cells, (three aircraft) in order to spread the force out for refueling. After refueling we had to fly a complex series of boxes, which took about an hour, to get the force back together. The twenty minute delay on the aborted tanker cell could have been enough to destroy the timing. (Authors note: Remember that 117 B-52's were over their targets within 13 minutes, which required exquisite timing.) Well, we did some quick and dirty flight planning, and Colonel McCarthy ordered the second wave leader to adjust his refueling schedule to rendezvous with follow-on tankers. It worked and the aborted tanker cell finally made it off and took the 2nd wave leader's instructions to complete an effective offload. The second wave leader was a Major LeBar, and it is to his credit that he got his cells refueled and back into the stream at the proper time, and in the proper sequence.

The force was together now, and we chased the setting sun westward. When it finally went down, we were confronted with a beautiful, clear, starry sky.

After nearly six hours of flying, we finally reached the coast of South Vietnam, and turned northward. As soon as we passed the DMZ, we began to get indications on the ECM gear that the enemy radars were looking at us, so we knew they would have ample warning in the target areas. We were flying almost due north, splitting the Gulf of Tonkin. I looked out the right front windscreen, and there was Hainan Island lit up like a Christmas Tree. I said; "Gee, we're awfully close to that dude! I was thinking out loud, and I remember that when I had flown my 100 F-4 missions, we had always avoided Hainan because the Chinese would launch Mig-19's out of there to engage us if we got within their controlled airspace. The Navigator must have sensed my concern, because he came back with; "Naw, we've got plenty of room". Out in front of us was the coastline of China. It too was lit up, and you could pick out all the little coastal towns, gleaming like a string of gems in the clear night air.

On our left was the coast of North Vietnam and, as we watched, we could see that the F-111's and A-6's had begun their attacks on the SAM sites. All of a sudden, you would see a flare-up of AAA, then the bombs would go off. I knew their times on target, and as I consulted my watch, it was comforting to note that they were right on time. The Navy had guaranteed us that they would keep the SAM sites around Haiphong busy. We had replied with; "Fine, but don't work them over too hard.....they're lousy shots, and if you get them all, they might be replaced by someone who is better!"

We cut short of the Chinese coast and headed inland. When we got to the northeast railway, we cut to the south and headed for our target, which was the Hanoi railyards, right across the street from Gia Lam Airport. We could really tell when we had reached the SAM lines, for they started coming up almost faster than we could count them. A SAM launch at night is quite a sight. There was a low undercast, so we couldn't actually see the ground. What we would see was a flash of light under the clouds, which was greatly diffused and spread by the clouds. It was almost like an explosion. Then, pretty soon, you would see this ball of fire come up through the clouds, accelerating at an amazing rate. You knew then that it was a SAM. What you didn't know, and often couldn't tell until it was too late, was whether or not it was ticketed for you, and, because of the convergence of the different waves, there was a startling number of them visible to us. I was pretty busy flying the airplane and keeping the cells together with the radio, so I didn't have time to get too worried about them. Colonel McCarthy, riding in the IP seat just behind and between the pilots, had time to count them...for awhile. By the time I made my 180 seconds to bomb release call, he had counted 26 in the air, visible to us in the windscreen. He gave up after that...they were just coming up too fast. We saw some triple A, but it really didn't concern us too much...it just wasn't that accurate. In fact, we were almost glad to see it. For some reason, they never seemed to fire AAA and SAMs at the same time, so when we saw the AAA, we knew we were getting a breather from the SAMs. They came close though. One that we didn't see coming couldn't have missed us by more than ten feet. It was just suddenly there and gone, but for a few seconds it was literally as bright as daylight in the cockpit. We were just damn lucky that the thing apparently malfunctioned and didn't go off when it was supposed to.

The intercom communications during the bomb run and just before and after made an interesting contrast with the first few missions. When we first went to Hanoi, getting a SAM shot at you was enough to raise everyone's voice a few octaves, and often you would hear the EW blurt out something like: **"PILOT! SAMTWELVEO'CLOCKTHREERINGS-COMINGTHISWAY!!!"** On the night of the 26th, I remember a call that went something like this; "Uh...Pilot, SAM...five o'clock, three and a half rings...uh...no biggie, press on." And on the bomb run, if you didn't know better, (by looking outside) you would have sworn you were on a normal RBS back in the states. The guys were cool personified as they commented; (Looking at the radar scope) "Yeah, there's the target...there's the offsets..O.K., no sweat" I guess it just goes to show you that you can adjust pretty quickly to any situations if you've had the training and experience.

But the strain sometimes manifested itself in spite of what a guy showed outwardly. My navigator, had been in headquarters, and had not been on a crew for about six years until he came to southeast Asia. He had been on my crew for about five months, and it was apparent that he had not lost any of his expertise, because he did an outstanding job as lead navigator. As we came off the target that night, he called; "Pilot, left turn, two six zero." Well, 260 degrees was to the right, of course. So, to jab him in the butt a little bit, (We were the same rank, and were often ribbing each other about our respective jobs.) I said; "You mean RIGHT TURN don't you Nav?"..."No, DAMMIT! I said LEFT TURN!"..."Uh, Nav, You want me to make a 360 degree turn to come around to two six zero?"...pregnant silence..."Uh, well, do whatever you want to!"...Nav, you want me to give you a rock to hold in one hand?" Well, that cracked eveyone up, coming as it did, just as we came off the target, with SAMs whizzing through the air all around us, and it really broke some of the tension.

As we came off the target, the sky to the northeast lit up with a tremendous flare, as a B-52 blew up in the air. We knew we were losing some, without even hearing the calls. When you eject, your beeper locator beacon on your survival radio automatically starts transmitting on the guard frequency. As I said, I had been in fighters, and had heard a few of them. But when you lose a B-52, and everyone gets out, there are six of them going simultaneously. And if you lose two or three in the same time period, the beeping is enough to drive you bananas! You can't shut it out, and you know you've lost a big one. Every now and then that sound will come back to me...like a song that reminds you of an event...I guess it'll haunt me forever.

While we were in the predetermined threat area, (a set of geographical coordinates) it was hard to keep track of all of my airplanes on the common radio frequency, since there was a lot of traffic concerning SAM launches, Mig calls, "I'm hit" calls, beepers, etc. So, based on my experience from my two previous Linebacker II missions, I came up with the following procedure: As each cell entered the threat area, they would go to a discreet frequency, which would allow the cell leader to keep track of his airplanes and to call threats that applied to them without interference. Upon leaving the threat area, they would go back to the common frequency and automatically check in with me. I asked them to keep it brief, and just give me: "As briefed, (if they had gotten their bombs on the target) out with three". (If they had their cell intact.) If they had lost one, or had some other problem, they were to elaborate. Well, they started checking in, and you could just feel everyone holding their breath as the reports came in. When the last cell checked in "as briefed, out with three", and we knew that we had gotten all the bombs on the target without losing anyone, I exclaimed; "SHIT HOT! Let's take em' home!" That really broke the tension, and you could hear all kinds of chatter up and down the radio net. After a few seconds, I asked them to cool it and we set power and climbed for our recovery altitude of 41,000, heading back to Andersen.

I was exhausted, and I gave the airplane to the co-pilot, settled back in the seat, and went to sleep. He woke me about three hours later, as we flew into the sunrise. We were pretty far back in the stream, due to our post-target position, and as far as we could see, over the horizon, there were sets of three contrails, crisscrossing as the cell navigators made their minute corrections. It was an impressive sight, and once again brought home to me the power of that raid."

The last Linebacker II sorties were flown on December 29, 1972. In the brief time that the campaign had lasted, the B-52's had dropped more than 49,000 bombs on the enemy homeland. They had destroyed or damaged over 1600 military structures and 373 pieces of railroad equipment. An estimated three million gallons of petroleum products were destroyed. The rail system was interdicted in at least 500 places, and imports from Russia and China were reduced from 160,000 tons to 30,000 tons per month. Additionally, enemy airfields were interdicted in at least ten separate places. No B-52's were lost to Migs, and B-52 gunners were credited with two confirmed Mig kills. Fifteen B-52's were lost during Linebacker II, (an overall loss rate of 2%) and 8 crewmembers lost their lives. 25 crewmembers are still carried as missing in action. Thirty three were captured and subsequently released.

The raids had taken their toll of the enemy defenses. In the last two raids, no B-52's were hit, and it was apparent that they were bombing the enemy homeland with virtual impunity at the end of the campaign.

Secretary of State Henry Kissinger stopped short of categorically crediting Linebacker II with ending U.S. participation in the war, but not by much. In his words; "There was a deadlock which was described in the middle of December, and there was a rapid movement when negotiations resumed on the technical level on January 3rd, and on the substantive level on January 8th. These facts have to be analyzed by each person for himself".

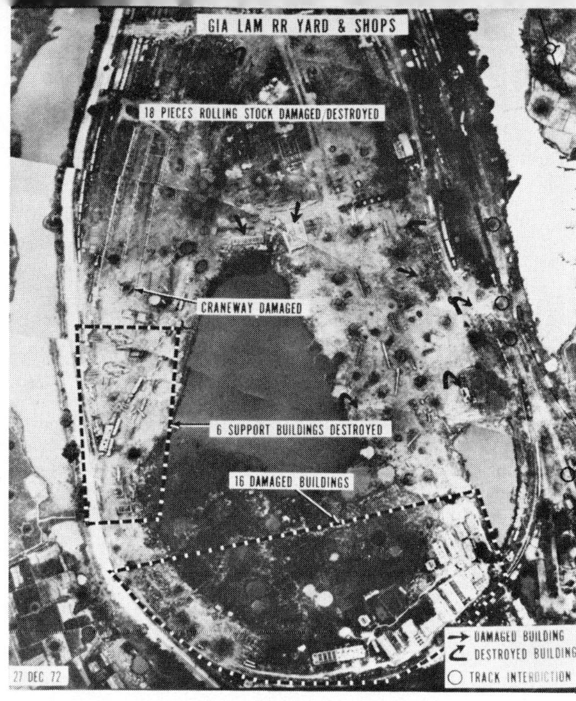

Precision of the high altitude radar bombing of the B-52's is demonstrated by before and after photos of the Hanoi Thermal Power Plant. Note the almost complete destruction of the target, with almost no damage to residential areas surrounding it. [left photos] Gia Lam RR Yard was struck on the 26 December mission. [right] [USAF]

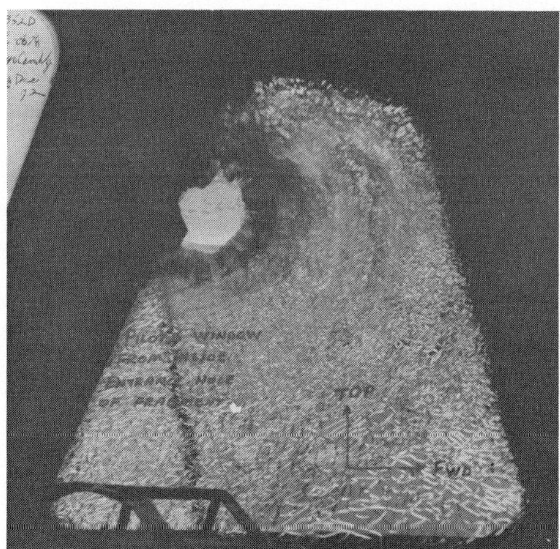

B-52's made the Kinh No RR Yard a wasteland. [left] B-52's were able to sustain major battle damage and still return to base, as evidenced by these photos. Left photo shows entrance hold made in pilot's window by SAM fragment, while right photo shows devastation of gunner's compartment by a near SAM detonation. [USAF]

The only B-52 to carry the sharkmouth into combat operated from Andersen AFB, Guam in 1972. It was so decorated by the ground crews, with the indulgence of 43rd Strategic Wing CO Col. James McCarthy. [BG James McCarthy]

Major Bill Stocker flew his 300th B-52 mission in November, 1972, and was appropriately hosed down upon de planeing. With him are Squadron Commander L/Col Maynard [left] and Wing Commander Col. McCarthy. [USAF via Maj. Bill Stocker]

KC-135 tanker of the 4104th Refueling Squadron, Korat RTAB, July, 1972. Unit was commanded by Col. James R. McCarthy. Possibly the only KC-135 ever to carry a sharkmouth. [BG James McCarthy]

Arc Light Memorial at Andersen AFB consists of plaque and permanently displayed B-52D. It commemorates the sacrifice of B-52 crews who did not return. Flanking the memorial are Lt. Gen. George H. McKee and Col. James R. McCarthy. [USAF]

B-52 Today

Twenty years after the Air Force took delivery of its first B-52; the Stratofortress remains an effective, if somewhat tired, weapons system. In its career, the B-52 has performed every mission it has been tasked with, some of which were never envisioned for it. SAC and the B-52 have outlived the limited war philosophy of the sixties, and are once again assuming the role of "the first team" in America's defense posture.

The "team" concept is emphasized by General Russell E. Dougherty, CINCSAC, whom I interviewed while doing research for this book. General Dougherty is justifiably proud of all of the people in SAC, and he gave a special mention to the tanker crews, whose aerial gas stations give the B-52's and FB-111's their worldwide reach.

While explaining the "TRIAD" concept of complementary retaliatory systems, he stressed the flexibility of the manned bomber. In a crisis the bombers can be launched and be kept on airborne alert almost indefinitely, then recalled when the situation cools. In this posture they are far less vulnerable than a fixed missile site, and they provide very graphic evidence of a nation's will to resist aggression. Missiles are the weaponry of conflagration. Bombers are the instruments of confrontation which will, hopefully, lead to negotiation and peaceful retrenchment. Both are vital to our survival as a free people, and our bomber force is in need of modernization. The B-52 has been a remarkable aircraft for a remarkable number of years, but its career is in the gloaming. The B-1 is on the horizon. Its acquisition will ensure continued viability for TRIAD, and allow the graceful retirement of the Stratofortress.

As this is written, SAC is hopeful of receiving the B-1, but they are also committed to maintaining their B-52 force for several years into the future. The professionalism and dedication of SAC people will add the necessary few years to the B-52's service life, and when it finally retires from the active inventory, the Stratofortress will have earned a special niche in the military aviation hall of fame.

I was fortunate enough to accompany a B-52 crew of the 97th Bomb Wing on a typical training mission from Blytheville AFB, Arkansas. These are my impressions of that mission.

Planning for the mission began the day before it was flown, and occupied all of the time of the crew, which consisted of Pilot Major John Ewing, Co-Pilots Lt. Leo Anthamatten and Lt. Dave Vandenburg, Radar Navigator Capt. Ian Robinson, Navigator Lt. Jerry Ledford, Electronics Warfare Officer Major Charles Moss, and Gunner MSgt James Carman.

Takeoff time was 0700, which meant getting the old biological clock turned on a couple of hours early for me. I met the crew in Base Operations at 0445, and they had already done a good deal of the day's work. The weather was balmy and the first gray light of dawn made its appearance as we boarded the crew bus for the ride to the flight line. SAC crews must have very special biological clocks, because they acted as though they got up in the middle of the night every day, as they made small talk while I was still trying to will my brain to middle-of-the-day awareness. Once we pulled up to the airplane, they were all business.

As soon as the bus had stopped, the crew chief came aboard and

Author [left] sits in on crew briefing for his B-52 mission.

B-52G engine start. [Author]

Taxiing to the active. [Author]

turned over the maintenance forms for B-52G AF Serial Number 59-2592 to the pilot. Major Ewing scanned them carefully, sharply questioning the crew chief about the idiosyncrasies of the airplane. We did not dismount the bus until he was satisfied that the airplane was airworthy.

I accompanied Lt. Vandenburg on the preflight walk around. He explained that his preflight was more a visual check for fuel or hydraulic leaks than anything else, since the real preflight inspection must be accomplished by the line crew, and takes several hours. You'd think that a cursory inspection such as ours could have been accomplished in five minutes. Not so. It would probably take five minutes just to walk around a B-52. Looking for leaks in all the possible places they could occur adds several more minutes, and by the time you're finished, you are more than ever impressed with the size of the Big Ugly.....uh.....Fella.

You climb into the BUF from a hatch directly under the crew compartments. Enroute to the flight deck, you pass through the cubbyhole occupied by the Navigator and Radar Navigator. (And the **very** spartan restroom facilities.) Up one more flight, and you're on the flight deck level. The EWO and Gunner sit about 15 feet behind the front office, facing to the rear. I sat in the Instructor Pilot seat, which is slightly behind and between the Pilot and Co-Pilot seats. I found my parachute and went about fitting it. Even when you know what you're doing with a parachute, getting one on in the crew compartment of the B-52 is no mean feat. As big as the airplane is, there isn't any room to spare in the crew compartment. In fact, you cannot stand upright.

Once settled, I watched the Pilot and Co-Pilot go through the preflight checklists. This entailed a great deal of passing back and forth of manuals and novelette-sized checklists as the preflight went on...and on...and on. Finally, as 0630 rolled around, it was time to start the engines. This took four hands and more checking and cross-checking as the eight throttles were manipulated to bring the J-57 engines to life.

With the big B-52 thrumming with energy, Major Ewing checked the operation of the stabilator trim, while the crew chief confirmed visually that the massive stab was where the trim control said it was. The last "before taxi" item was checked off the check list and we were ready to go.

The control tower cleared us to taxi and the throttles were advanced. Since you sit well forward of the landing gear, there is a distinct impression of overshooting your turns on the ground, and just as I was beginning to wonder if we were going to taxi into Base Operations, the nose swung majestically to the right and we headed down the taxiway. On the taxiway, the pilots disengaged the crosswind gear position wheel and tested it while we moved toward the active runway. This is one of the most interesting features of the B-52. It allows the pilot to compute the correct crab angle for a given crosswind direction and velocity, then line up the airplane into the wind, while the landing gear tracks straight down the white line on takeoff or landing. It is absolutely eerie to be taxiing straight down the white line, while the nose swings several degrees right then left of center. When the crew was satisfied that the system was working properly, they set in the precomputed angle for our takeoff.

We stopped short of the active and watched another B-52 returning from a night-long mission make a perfect landing and roll-out. It was 0652, but when the flight plan says 0700 takeoff, you wait until 0700 to takeoff. As I was to observe several times during the mission, SAC crews shoot for

Major John Ewing, USAF. [Author]

perfection, and that means accomplishing all phases of their mission "on the hack".

At 0700 we were rolling. This was a water-injection takeoff, so the Co-Pilot adjusted the throttles to a precomputed setting. At the proper moment, the Pilot hit the water injection and there was an added burst of power from the engines, which caused a hell of a lot more noise, and a noticeable increase in acceleration. The increased acceleration didn't snap many necks, but the fact that it was noticeable at all was impressive considering our takeoff weight of over 401,000 pounds. Meantime, down in "the well", the Navigator had been timing our takeoff roll. When we reached the precomputed S-1 time, he called a go for takeoff, and the Pilot called "committed" as we attained S-1 speed. We unstuck at 147 knots, and the Co got the gear up as we began to climb. The flaps came up slowly. Shortly after takeoff, the 1,200 gallons of water ran out, and the loss of thrust at this point was much more impressive than I expected. The throttles were firewalled and the nose lowered to gain climb speed.

The weather was VFR, but Jack Ewing was already hunkered down, flying by the gauges, as departure control handed us off to the center and we climbed toward flight level 370. We were on course for Tyndall AFB, Florida, where we were to act as target for an F-106 Interceptor mission. I heard a clonk...clonk...clonk clonk clonk clonk, which seemed to be coming from directly underfoot. Since nobody else seemed to be paying any attention, I didn't worry about it, but my curiosity finally got the upper hand, and I had to ask. I was told that it was our radar antenna cycling, looking at the ground, and at possible weather, or other airplanes. We were required to wear helmet and parachute for the takeoff, but Jack Ewing told me that I could now go to the headset, which is a lot more comfortable than the fibreglass hat. When I made the switch, I was amazed at the noise in the cockpit...I think you'd have a tough time carrying on a conversation on anything but the intercom, as those eight Pratt & Whitney's really crank out some decibels!

As we passed FL310, I heard Center advise an L-1011 airliner of our presence, at his 10 o'clock. A few seconds later the airline pilot asked the controller what sort of airplane we were. There was the inflection of someone who is sharing a choice bit of information when he replied that it was a B-52 that was bearing down on the airliner. (No, I don't know why...I can only know what I heard.)

When we arrived in the Tyndall area, it was back to the helmet and (grunt) parachute. We were advised by Whetstone Control that the fighter was having radio glitches, and would be late in getting up. In the meantime, he would give us vectors to troll up and down the coast. Ten minutes passed, then the controller advised us of further delay. Jack told the controller that he wanted vectors to get us to the exit point of the area on the hour. (Ever faithful to the flight plan.) The controller rogered that... then added a postscript of his own for our edification: "Hob Two Four, be advised that "Fighter Pilots Do It Better"...but they can only do it better when they can get it up!" Everyone got a chuckle out of that, since fighter pilots seem prone to come up with cute slogans, and the former is one of their favorites.

The fighter finally got off, and we heard his controller giving him bearing and distance vectors to us. He had time for two head-on passes, with stern re-attacks. It felt almost like World War II, watching him come at us. Of course, we were a lot higher, (40,000 feet) and the rate of closure was much faster, but it still had the flavor. The first thing you'd spot was the fighter's contrail, which had the appearance of a squiggly, hard white cloud. Then he would appear and before you knew what was happening, the distinctive planform of the 106 was belly up to you as he broke and dove under you. The BUF is limited by age and inclination when it comes to evasive action, but we made some attempts. The real weapons against a fighter are your ECM and Chaff...and, if he is stupid enough to press in close on a stern attack, the battery of four 50's mounted in the tail and radar directed. Our gunner claimed a "kill" on the last pass, as the chaff apparently fooled the 106 pilot momentarily and he buzzed past the tail, close enough for a 50 caliber shower. (Fifty caliber aerial gunnery might seem a little old hat in the age of supersonic fighters, but when the BUF's were challenged by Migs over North Vietnam, the final score was; BUF's: 2 - Migs: zip.)

Out of Whetstone control area, we headed back north for our rendezvous with "Cut Nine Eight", the KC=135 tanker who would aerial refuel for us. We were at 27,000 feet, in layer of stratus. Visibility was about two to three miles...sometimes less. The radar navigator was calling distance and bearing to the tanker continuously. The KC-135 was flying the "track", a racecourse shaped path in the sky. If we were on time, he would roll out of a turn right in front of us, ready to pass us the JP-4.

Another testimonial to SAC flight planning. We spotted the tanker just as he rolled out of his turn, two miles in front of us. This was one of the more impressive portions of the flight for me. We closed on the tanker rapidly, then matched his speed as the "boomer" got his flying umbilical out. Then he cleared us into the contact position. We moved in, and with such ease it almost seemed anti-climactic, contact was made with an audible double "clunk". The refueling slipway is almost directly over the IP seat, so I had no trouble confirming the very positive contact.

The B-52 autopilot has a "refueling mode" which allows control movements that almost seem obscene, and Jack was really working to maintain contact as we took on 35,000 lbs. of JP-4. Aerial refueling has become a taken-for-granted adjunct to air operations, but you have to experience the sight of that boom waving around a foot in front of your windscreen to appreciate the skill required to make it the routine happening that it is. I was beginning to appreciate the pride General Dougherty had shown in his tanker crews. Not only do the pilots have to fly a rock-steady path, but the boom operator has to handle his lance-like probe with the delicacy of a surgeon. We had only had the most moderate turbulence, and I had decided that I wouldn't like to be watching the operation if things really got bumpy.

After we dropped off the tanker, we turned and headed for Southern North Carolina, where we would let down for our "Olive Branch Route". (This is the low level navigation and bombing course, which used to be called "Oil Burner Route", a name which made some visual sense, what with the great black clouds of smoke those eight engines would belch at low level. Why they changed the name to "Olive Branch" I don't know, although I could make several guesses.)

The letdown was gradual and precise. The checkpoints rolled by, right on time, while we kept the center advised of our progress. There was an almost continual conversation with the FAA controllers as we progressed, and the Co-Pilot was kept plenty busy changing frequencies and looking outside to verify our position on the chart. We were south of Fort Bragg, North Carolina, and I mused that the last time I had seen this view of this terrain it was from the open door of a C-119, while assigned to the 82nd Airborne Division 18 years previously. (I can guarantee you that the ground wasn't going by anywhere near as fast.) We roared southwesterly across South Carolina and finally turned west on our bomb run. We were now at 1,000 feet and clipping along at 340 kts. It was only relatively bumpy, so I could almost enjoy the sensation of speed as the checkpoints disappeared under the nose. I wondered how the locals reacted to sight of something this big, going this fast, as it blotted out the sun. Even though the Olive Branch Routes are set and frequently used, I can't imagine anyone getting used to the simultaneous impact on the senses that 200 tons of unmitigated power roaring along at something near 400 miles per hour would make. We made two runs on the low level target are, then headed back toward Blytheville, climbing towards flight level 310. We were 6½ hours into the mission, and the navigator had us on time within a minute. I was still impressed.

We made some detours getting through the front that the weather man had promised us wouldn't get to Blytheville until after we had returned, but which, with the unerring canniness of all bad weather had decided to accelerate and meet us halfway home. Once through the front, the visibility was practically unlimited.

I spotted the Mississippi meandering south as we approached Blytheville from the east. We droned over the base at 20,000 feet as the pilots got out their charts and prepared to make the approach. Over the VOR and turn back to the east. Get the gear and flaps out. Turn right and line up with runway one seven for a long final. Set the crab angle on the landing gear...tower clears us to land. Approach speed 145 knots. Runway coming up. Jack plants it so smoothly that I am glad that the runway has some bumps in it...I'd never know we were down. I compliment him on the landing, and he says that all B-52 landings are like that. But I think I know better...he just did a fantastic job all day long, and this was a fitting climax to the flight.

EVS [Electro-Optical Sensor] equipped B-52H. SAC tactics call for B-52's to go to war at low level, and all B-52's are equipped with curtains which can be pulled over windows to protect the crew from nuclear flash. EVS provides the means, through low-light level TV and infrared sensors, to view the terrain without looking outside. [USAF]

Cockpit of EVS equipped B-52 [left] shows off TV screens. Engine instruments are grouped in center of panel, while flight instruments are immediately in front of the pilots. Communications panel is out of sight, overhead between seats. Note substantial size of stabilator trim wheel. [left of throttles] EVS infrared and low light level TV sensors under the nose of B-52H. Low level camouflage is standard two tone green and tan upper and gloss white heat reflective lower surfaces. [USAF]

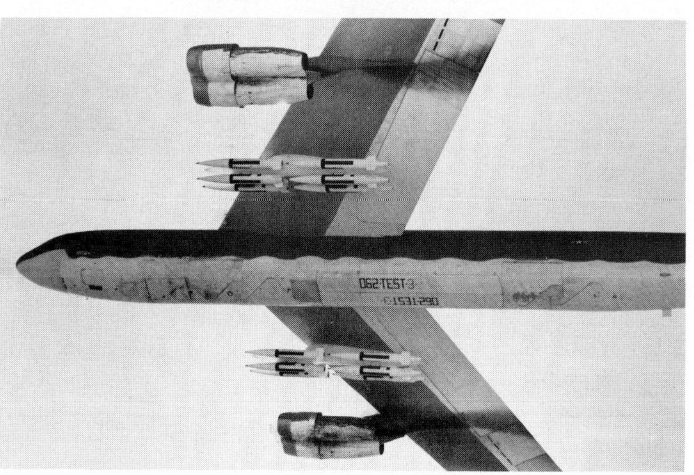

Most up-to-date version of the B-52 is this "H" model, equipped with EVS and SRAM missiles. It is this combination that will have to uphold the manned bomber role of TRIAD until the B-1 [hopefully] becomes operational in the late 70's. AGM-69A SRAM is over 14 feet long, weighs nearly 2,000 lbs. and has a speed of mach 2.5 over a maximum range of 100 miles. It is extremely maneuverable, having 180 degree turn capability. "G" and "H" models carry up to 20 SRAMs. Even with the introduction of the B-1 into the inventory, the B-52 will remain in the operational inventory well into the 1980's. Some B-52's may even be around to celebrate their 30th anniversary of operational use, making them one of the most cost-effective weapons systems in modern history.

Vietnam Studies Grou

squadron/signal's Vietnam Studies Group

6010
$6.95
PHANTOM II
A Pictorial History of the McDonnell Douglas F-4 Phantom II
by Lou Drendel
squadron/signal publications

Vietnam Studies Group
$8.95
AIR WAR
over
Southeast Asia
A Pictorial Record
Vol. 2 1967-1970
By Lou Drendel

Coming Soor